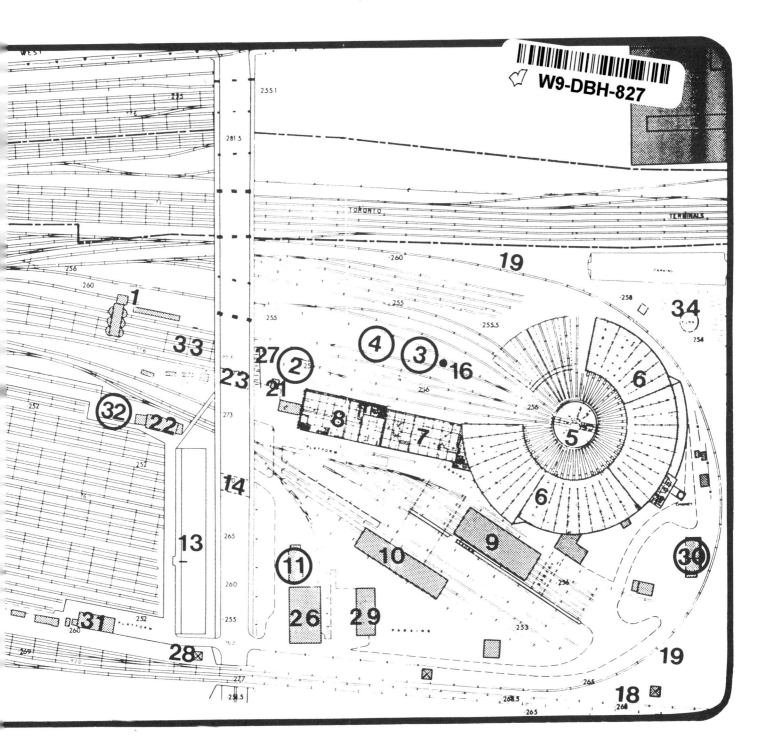

25. Yard Office
26. Telegraph Stores
27. Stair Case, Spadina Bridge
28. Gate House
29. Telegraph Storage
30. Pintsch Gas
31. Ice House
32. Charcoal Shed
33. Fueling Deck
34. Fuel Tank
35. Car Washer
36. Miscellaneous structures

Map from:
Railway Heritage Study In Toronto
Historica Research Limited, 1983

KEEP 'EM ROLLING

THE STORY OF
TORONTO'S SPADINA ROUNDHOUSE

AS SEEN THROUGH THE CAMERA OF
HARRY WATSON
1923 – 1966

BY
RON WATSON

Canadian Cataloguing in Publication Data

Watson, Ron, 1932-
    Keep 'em rolling

Bibliography: p.
ISBN 0-919822-63-0

1. Railroads – Ontario – Toronto – Roundhouses.
2. Railroads – Ontario – Toronto – History.
I. Title.

TF296.W37 1984   385'.09713'541   C84-098830-3

Published in Canada by
THE BOSTON MILLS PRESS,
98 Main St.,
Erin, Ontario, N0B 1T0

Typeset by Linotext Inc., Toronto, Ontario
Printed by John Deyell Co., Toronto, Ontario

The Boston Mills Press gratefully acknowledges the assistance
of the Canada Council, the Ontario Arts Council and the Office of the
Secretary of State.

Winners of the
Heritage Canada
Communications Award

American Association
for State and Local History
Award Winner

Mountain 6066, Northern 6404 and the Vanderbilt tender of Hudson 5701 line up with the water tower as a backdrop.

The 6537, streamlined and new in July of 1958, is ready for a run on a balmy summer day. Harry Watson, in his summer fatigues, looks like he'd like to take off with her!

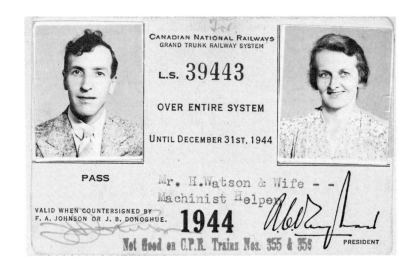

This book is dedicated to
my Mother
and to the memory of
my Dad

Harry and Beatrice Watson at "Canadian National Railways Night,"
Union Lodge 1252, Veteran's Presentations, 1969,
which was held in the Oak Room at Toronto's Union Station.

Bullet-Nosed Betty 6064 belches smoke as she passes under the Spadina bridge.

Plenty of hustle and bustle in the ash pits. Looking east toward the roundhouse from Spadina bridge, we can see great clouds of smoke drifting over the yards across the city. The stores building is on the right.

FOREWORD
Notes from the Past

"Ron, keep these negatives of steam engines and diesel. They're valuable and you may meet someone very interested in steam engines."

"These are very good negatives of steam. Engine 6261, 5701, 6060, 6404; wood burner and diesel."

These notes, written on a tattered brown envelope, were happened-upon when trying to decide what to do with several cartons containing negatives, albums of pictures, and photographic equipment in my home a few years ago. The lifetime hobby of my Dad was represented here, and I didn't know where to begin. A few well-placed phone calls confirmed that the negatives were indeed valuable, but what to do with them was not resolved until later, when the world of railways gradually revealed itself to me.

Harry Watson spent over forty-three years on the Canadian National Railways, and during interviews with his co-workers, it was said that, "These pictures may be Harry's finest hour in railroading." Hours of research, and hours of interviews, led to the making of this book.

Choosing the title of the book, *Keep 'em Rolling*, was not a difficult task, as it is what my Dad told me he did when he went to work. Although unofficial, the motto was widely used by roundhouse workers, as confirmed by recent interviews with Harry's fellow employees. An adaptation of the motto was used in the 1950's by the "Canadian Brotherhood of Railway Employees and Other Transportation Workers," which included members of Unions that governed the boilermakers, machinists, blacksmiths, tinsmiths, electricians, carmen, and pipefitters that worked at Spadina. Like their motto at work, "Keep 'em Rolling," the members applied it to their Brotherhood, "To Keep It Rolling."*

Harry Watson gave life to his photographs of locomotives. A puff of smoke here and a shot of steam there were the exclamation points that confirmed to the viewer that these locomotives had personality. His eye for a picture, and methodical attention to detail, have provided us with a chronological record of the panorama of railroading during an exciting period of its history.

The photographs in this book came from my father's collection of over 700 black and white negatives of railway operations, and were taken primarily at the following locations:

1. Spadina shops,
2. The entrance to the train sheds of the old and new Union Stations,
3. Danforth Station, Toronto,
4. The Canadian National Exhibition,
5. On the main lines to Toronto.

An attempt to glimpse through the window of the past into an era of steam and diesel locomotives, as well as at the men who maintained them, is the purpose of this book. Only a moment of railroading history is portrayed; a moment that is fast becoming absorbed by concrete, steel, glass and new technology as the modern city moves on. In recording these moments of human struggle, friendship, laughter, pleasure and hard work, an overriding feeling filters through of the pride and personal satisfaction which the men had in their work; and pride in the company for which they worked. My Dad always said that, "The people in the roundhouse are the most important in the railway world," because they knew that it was on them that everything depended to 'Keep 'em Rolling.'

Canadian Transport, 1954

Ron Watson,
Agincourt, Ontario,
May, 1984.

Harry Watson beside locomotive 5700.

HARRY WATSON

Harry Watson was born in the town of Burnley, Lancashire, England on August 18, 1901, and attended school there. His father, William Henry, and his younger brother Willie, worked on the railroad in England.

Harry played the trombone in a local band and was in the Boy Scouts. When the time came for him to begin working, he wanted to join the railroad like his father, but was instead encouraged to get a job at the weaving mill in town.

When the economy deteriorated in England, Harry emigrated to Canada and arrived in Toronto, Ontario in 1923. Although the job situation was not much better in Canada, he did secure a position with the Canadian National Railways which became his permanent place of employment.

He grew to love Toronto as his new home and in 1928 returned to England to marry Beatrice Annie Robinson, who accompanied him back to Toronto after a honeymoon in London. They purchased a house on Parkmount Road in Toronto's east end in September, 1932, which became their only permanent address. During the early years, Beatrice and Harry were active members of the Anglican Church of the Nativity and remained so until its closing.

It was in the early 1920's that Harry bought himself a Number 2 Brownie Kodak camera in which he used a number 120 film. In later years he progressed to a Kodak Vigilant Junior 620, which featured a delay timer that allowed him to appear in many of his own photographs.

A camera became his constant companion on his many travels, and especially at the CNR Spadina roundhouse where he worked as a machinist's helper. Harry saw and recorded the many changes that modern technology brought; from steam in the early 1920's, to the first experimental diesel in 1927, and back again to steam until the modern diesel came into being.

Recording these changes became an absorbing hobby which occupied many hours of Harry's time, and which included the developing and printing of his own pictures. He systematically entered his photographs in albums and filed negatives from 1923 onwards.

As an employee of the CNR, Harry had a pass for the entire system. He and Beatrice took advantage of the opportunity to travel and did so extensively, not only on local trips through Ontario, but throughout Canada and the United States. They returned many times to England where most of their family had remained.

At their home in Toronto, Beatrice and Harry enjoyed many hours in their back garden, which was admired by many for its beauty. Harry Watson enjoyed his home and his city. He never owned a car. He walked miles and miles, his camera recording things and events that interested him as he went. By walking, he was able to observe and capture life in the city as it was, life which many were beginning to miss as the automobile sped them quickly over the wide panorama of the growing metropolis. The railway took him to where he wanted to go. He worked for the railway and was proud of it. It served him and he served it — a railway man through and through.

Harry officially retired from active railroading with the Canadian National Railways on August 31, 1966, after over forty-three years of service. In a retirement which was very active, he always managed to go back to the roundhouse to see that everything was running smoothly. Failing health did not deter him, and he made what turned out to be his last visit there accompanied by his son Ron and grandson Chris. While others wore modern safety hats, no one would dare suggest that Harry wear one. He was one of the "old-timers" and proud of being a true "Gentleman of the Spadina Roundhouse."

Harry Watson passed away peacefully on Christmas Day, 1977.

Harry Watson's first camera, a Number 2 Brownie Kodak, took the earliest photographs which appear in this book.

The delay timer on Harry's Kodak Vigilant Junior allowed him to appear in many of his own photographs.

POSED IN A TEN WHEELER

*A young Harry Watson poses in the cab of Ten Wheeler 1567, formerly Grand Trunk Railway
324, which was built in 1901 and retired in March, 1936.*

A BRIEF HISTORY OF THE SPADINA RAILWAY LANDS

Spadina, a railroading name of prominence in North America, is a far cry from the original Spadina associated with wealth and elegance in early Toronto, Ontario. The street was laid out in 1836 as a park drive from Lot Street (now Queen Street), and was intended to go as far north as Dr. W.W. Baldwin's Georgian country estate (in the region of present day Casa Loma). Below Queen Street, Spadina Avenue was called Brock Street until 1884. Since those days, the wide avenue has become lined with industry, fading into a maze of railway tracks where the CNR's Toronto Spadina roundhouse is tucked away out of view of the general public.

Although this book deals primarily with the Canadian National Railways' lands and facilities as they appear to-day, many of the buildings in Harry Watson's early photographs were in existence long before the property came into CNR ownership.

The Toronto, Simcoe & Huron Railway was the first on the Toronto scene in 1853, purchasing 4 acres of land for its terminus to the west of Spadina (Brock St.) for the grand sum of $100. This pioneer Ontario railway was reorganized as the Northern Railway in 1858.

Meanwhile, the Grand Trunk Railway had finally arrived at the Don River in 1856, and continued to the eastern side of Spadina Ave in 1857, where it built its own unique domed roundhouse facility. The legacy of buildings left by the Northern Railway were added to the Grand Trunk in 1888, and all were subsequently merged into the Canadian National Railways in 1923.

None of these early buildings exist today, but many were still on the property in 1923 when Harry Watson joined the CNR. They continued to be used until construction of the modern Spadina roundhouse and shops in 1927-28.

Northern Railway yards west of Spadina Avenue (Brock St.)

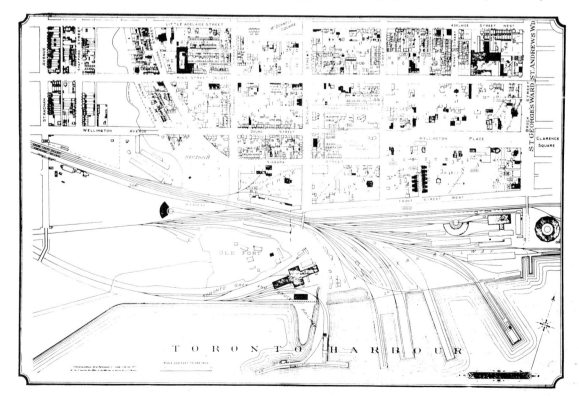

One of the earliest views of the Northern Railway's Toronto yards and engine facilities, seen from Bathurst Street looking east, circa 1860. The original Spadina (Brock St.) bridge can be seen crossing the Grand Trunk main line on the left. Clearly visible are the Northern Railway's roundhouse and machine shop, with the domed roof of the GTR roundhouse peeking over top in the distance. — The Boston Mills Press collection.

Grand Trunk yards east of Spadina Avenue (Brock St.)

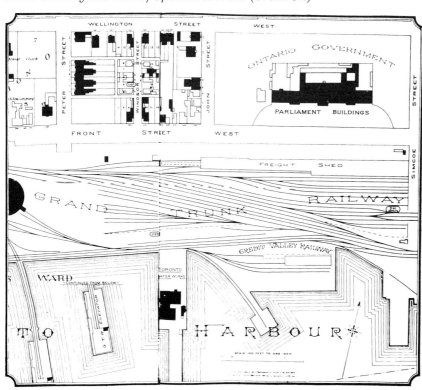

The Northern Railway's machine shop and roundhouse complex, looking southwest from the Spadina bridge, circa 1860. — The Boston Mills Press collection.

An artist's impression of Toronto's railway lands as they appeared looking northeast from the harbour wharves in 1876. The original Spadina bridge can be clearly seen to the left of the picture.

The Northern Railway's roundhouse is out of view to the left, but it and the shop buildings, which are visible to the left of the bridge, were familiar to Harry Watson during his first years on the railway.

To the right (east) of the bridge are the two roundhouses of the Grand Trunk Railway, basically on the same location as today's Spadina roundhouse and shops. Both GTR roundhouses had been replaced by the time of Harry Watson's arrival in 1923, engine servicing being undertaken in the "long shop." — Metropolitan Toronto Library photo T10279.

Another view of Toronto's railway lands at the foot of Spadina, as they appeared in 1884 looking west from John Street. The original Spadina bridge appears behind the two roundhouses. —Metropolitan Toronto Library photo T10362.

An undated view, probably in the early 1900's, showing the original Spadina bridge looking north. By this time the old shops of the Northern Railway, seen on the left, had become part of the Grand Trunk system. —Metropolitan Toronto Library photo T30205.

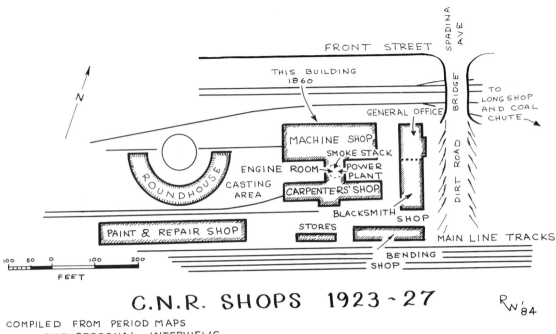

FRONT STREET

SPADINA AVE

THIS BUILDING 1860

GENERAL OFFICE

TO LONG SHOP AND COAL CHUTE

N

MACHINE SHOP

SMOKE STACK

ENGINE ROOM

POWER PLANT

ROUNDHOUSE

CASTING AREA

CARPENTERS' SHOP

BLACKSMITH SHOP

BRIDGE

DIRT ROAD

PAINT & REPAIR SHOP

STORES

MAIN LINE TRACKS

100 50 0 100 200

FEET

BENDING SHOP

C.N.R. SHOPS 1923-27

RW '84

COMPILED FROM PERIOD MAPS
AND PERSONAL INTERVIEWS

THE LONG SHOP

The original Northern Railway roundhouse to the west of Spadina was built to suit the needs of the ten locomotives that were used by the Northern at that time. By the 1920's, it had become a repair depot used only for yard engines, which measured in length approximately the same as the old Northern passenger engines. As for other uses, it was merely a storage area for parts and supplies. The north side of this roundhouse, immediately west of the old Northern turntable, was where early CNR crews repaired later locomotive models such as Consolidations and Mikados.

Just before the present roundhouse was constructed in 1927-28, the old GTR "Long Shop" was the main centre of activity for locomotive maintenance and repair. It was a frame structure approximately 250 feet long by 40 feet wide and housed three tracks. An open slot down the centre of the roof allowed smoke from the engines to escape. During the winter it was heated by three potbellied stoves, and the men were required to shovel coal from the locomotive tenders to fuel the stoves. Those with firsthand experience have said that three feet away from the stove, you were roasting, and ten feet away you were freezing. The pits, just over 3 feet deep, were always wet and icy in the winter, and damp and cold in the summer.

Herb Gough related some of the miserable conditions under which the railroaders worked in those days. To have some measure of warmth in which to work on the engines, it was necessary to keep all the doors closed. Lighting the engines to get them ready for main line passenger service created so much smoke, that moving about became impossible without a small coal oil torch. It was necessary to shout a constant warning to avert a collision with someone coming from the opposite direction. The glow from the potbellied stoves might give you some idea of which dirt path to follow, but one slip from the path and you would land in the pits. Ventilation was inadequate all year around, and most of the time it was necessary to just grin and bear it!

The coal chute provides a vantage point for Harry Watson's camera as he looks east through the lens to the John Street bridge in 1924. Notice the smoke seeping out of the ventilation slots on the long shop roof, and the smoke jacks for the potbellied stoves. The tip of the old Union Station tower can just be seen through the steam in the centre of the picture.

Looking east from the door of the ex-Grand Trunk long shop in 1924, a railroader looks back as he sits on a storage box beside a dispatch telephone. The John Street bridge is in the centre, with coach yards to the left and the main line to the right. The old Union Station tower can be seen in the background through the centre span of the bridge.

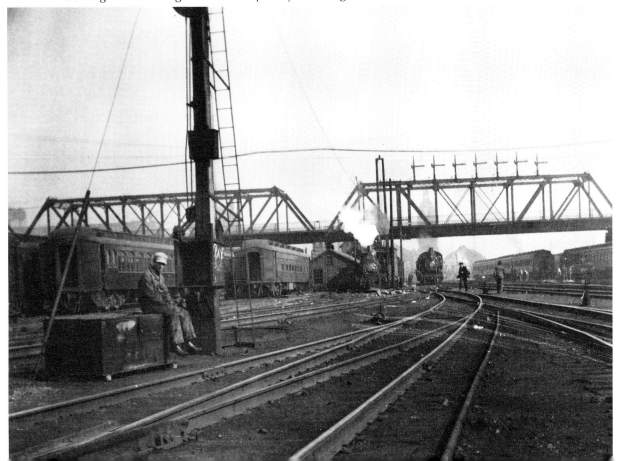

MOGULS AT THE LONG SHOP

Grand Trunk Railway 1279, later to become CN 815, is beside the old long shop building on the right. The long shop was demolished in 1926-27 to make room for the new roundhouse. Grand Trunk's wooden water tower forms a backdrop to CN 2531 on the left.
GTR 1279 was built in 1904 and retired in April, 1936.

Here the engineer and fireman pose in the cab of CN 765, formerly GTR 1228. The 765 was built in 1902 and retired in July, 1935.

The 810 sports Harry Watson in its cab, Davey Curran on the ground, and an unidentified fellow worker in the cab door.

CN 810, formerly GTR 1429, sits just outside of the long shop. Davey Curran stands at ease on the cowcatcher while the hose draws a steam exhaust draft until steam power blows the stack. The 810 was built in 1903 and retired in July, 1935.

WOODEN WATER TOWER

Bobby Taylor tells how Lake Ontario nearly had a subsidiary in the Spadina Yards! George Burleigh, machinist, Eddy O'Brien, helper, and Bobby Taylor who was then the roustabout, were working the night shift. Bobby was given the job of maintaining the level in the water tower so that the tenders could be filled up in the morning. On seeing the need to bring up the water level, Bobby walked the short distance to the willow bush at the edge of Lake Ontario where the water pumps were located, and turned them on. Returning to the ash pit shanty, and seeing the shanty men both asleep, he sat down beside them and fell asleep too. Waking to a noise like thunder, he opened the door to the shanty and beheld water coming out of the top of the water tank like Niagara Falls. He ran all the way back to the willow bush to shut the pumps off, but by then a huge lake had formed and it took quite a while for the yard to dry up.

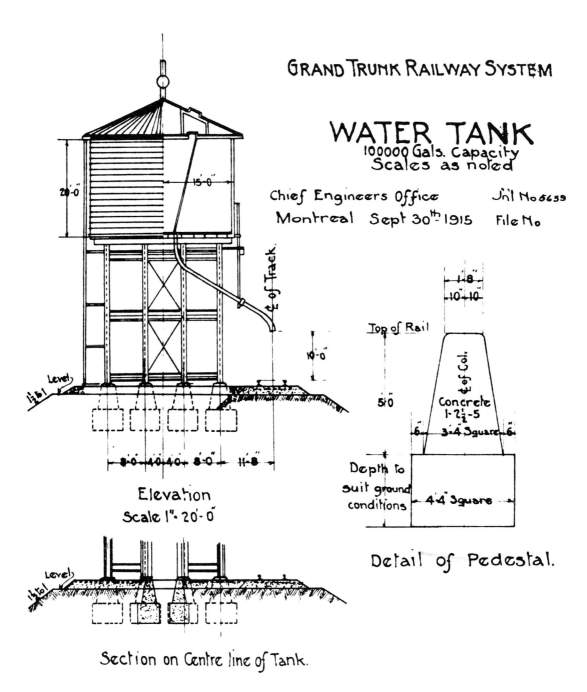

GRAND TRUNK RAILWAY SYSTEM

WATER TANK
100000 Gals. Capacity
Scales as noted

Chief Engineers Office   Jn'l No 5639
Montreal Sept 30th 1915   File No

Elevation
Scale 1" - 20'-0"

Detail of Pedestal.

Section on Centre line of Tank.

Steam and smoke obscure this 1924 view taken from the old Spadina bridge facing east. Left to right: a yard engine, long shop (with two engines in front), wooden coal chute, water tower, boiler room, bunk house with classroom and turntable.

This 1924 photograph was taken by Harry Watson from the coal shute, looking west towards the old Grand Trunk turntable and wooden water tower. Spadina, when it was still a dirt road, leads the way up the hill in front of the old Northern Railway blacksmith shop. A Consumer's Gas tank can be seen in the right background, behind the Bathurst Street bridge. Note that much additional filling and land reclamation has been undertaken at the harbour since the pre-1900 views.

THE BULL GANG

The first job for many who began their career with the Canadian National Railways in 1923 was with the bull gang. It was often the only job available, while waiting for an opening to apprentice in the machine shop or the roundhouse.

The duties of the men in the bull gang included all the tough, heavy, dirty and menial tasks which were available in abundance in the railway yards. Some of the tasks included breaking up the coal in winter, unloading lumber, moving heavy railway equipment, or even carrying sixty to seventy pound boxes of water softener from the Spadina shops to Union Station when someone forgot to order it for the water in the tenders. Coal heaving and digging trenches are to mention but a few of the other jobs, and team work was necessary for survival. Heavy, dirty work was their lot and that's why the men came to be known as the "Bull Gang."

In 1923-24 the average working day began at 7 a.m. and continued to 6 p.m. Monday to Friday, and 7 a.m. to 1 p.m. on Saturday. After being accepted as an apprentice, a person could expect to earn fifteen cents per hour.

Here the bull gang is leaning against a pile of lumber that they have just unloaded from a freight car, in Harry's first year on the railway in 1923. The building to the right is the west end of the old Northern Rly. machine shop, with a smaller building attached. This was put on especially for three female clerks who worked in the office. In order to use the facility, they had to travel through the main office, the machine and rail shops, then go outside and turn the corner to arrive at this little restroom. Incidentally, the men's restroom was kept under constant surveillance by an old chap who took your name when you went in and checked you off as you came out. No longer than seven minutes was allowed for a visit. Company rules!

Left to right—Hats on! Ernie Shewbridge, Davey Curran, Al Minister, Leslie Chapman, Sid Cope, Harry Watson, unidentified crane operators.

Left to right—Hats off! Tommy Haddon, Sid Cope, Jack Cope, Harry Watson, Davey Curran, Jim Beattie, Sammy Harris, unidentified.

ON DISPLAY

This locomotive was used for historical display by the CNR during the years 1925 to 1927. Restored at the Stratford shops, she appeared with various smokestacks as GTR 2194, GTR 169 and T&N 269.

Number 269 had no connection with the Toronto and Nipissing Railway, other than the name which seems to have been picked at random, perhaps for its pioneer flavour. Manufactured by the Canadian Locomotive Company in Kingston, Ontario in 1883, she was retired in October, 1929.

This photograph was taken prior to May, 1927 when the new Spadina bridge was opened. Forming a backdrop to the 269 is the old Northern (Grand Trunk) machine shop, which was demolished in 1927.

SPADINA AVENUE BRIDGE

In May, 1927, a new Spadina Avenue bridge was opened to traffic. It replaced the original bridge, which spanned just a few tracks south of Front Street, and became a major transportation route by linking Toronto to its alienated waterfront. The railroaders used it daily to get to work, and over the years it provided an ideal vantage point for Harry Watson to capture the activity of the Spadina yards below.
—Photo from Canadian Railway & Marine World, *June 1927.*
—Metropolitan Toronto Library.

COACH YARD

The passenger cars shown here in the early 1930's are at the stub end of the coach yard, which had capacity for 256 cars. The ice house at the right held 50 tons of ice. The commissary and car department building can be seen on the left.

SPADINA—A BIRD'S EYE VIEW

Harry Watson photographed this series of pictures when the present facilities were new in 1928, from the top of the floodlight systems which were mounted on 120 foot steel towers. The four to seven lights with reflectors varied from 14 to 23 inches in diameter, with wattage of from 780 to 1,000. It was stated that the cost of installation, maintenance and current consumed was less than what would be required by the very large number of small lights which would otherwise be used. It has also been said over the years that the tops of the steel towers were the best spot in town to view the annual Canadian National Exhibition fireworks display.

Looking southwest to Fleet Street and the waterfront. In the foreground is the roof of the store's building and the tracks to the coach shop. The bunkhouse and the telegraph stores building are at the left edge of the photograph. Immediately beyond the Spadina bridge is the roof of the commissary and car department building.

The bunkhouse was a two-storey brick structure (now demolished) with sleeping accommodation for 40 men. Also included in the house was a lunch room, reading room, shower and tub baths.

The commissary and car department building on the west side of the Spadina bridge is a two-storey brick and concrete structure, 368'2'' long by 50'2'' wide. The car department alone is 145'1'' by 50'2'' and accommodates 256 passenger cars with associated facilities.

THE ROUNDHOUSE

The heart of all railway facilities is the roundhouse, for it is to the roundhouse that the locomotives are brought, depleted and worn from their journey, to be serviced and sent out again, gleaming and ready for another run.

Today it's diesels, but first it was steam; and dirt, grime, grease and smoke were an undesirable constant in the environment. To the men who worked at the roundhouse, this was a part of the job which had to be either laughed off or ignored.

There are 36 stalls in the Spadina roundhouse, eight of which are shop stalls 130 feet long, the other 28 being 110 feet long. Nine spaces were provided for future expansion which was never realized, and were used for storage only. Stall 36 is shown to the left of the photograph, and fire walls can be seen between stalls 28-29, and 18-19. Not shown in the picture are those between stalls 8-9. The building at the top left of the photograph is the John Street Pumping Station on the City of Toronto Waterworks property.

TURNTABLE

The turntable is 100 feet long and of the twin-span type. This style eliminates the necessity of balancing the load over the centre of the table and reduces the turning time to a minimum. The feature is especially advantageous in turning dead locomotives, or equipment which does not propel itself. The table is also equipped with an electric drum for handling dead equipment and is approached by fifty tracks, five of which are running tracks and the remainder being locomotive house and storage tracks.

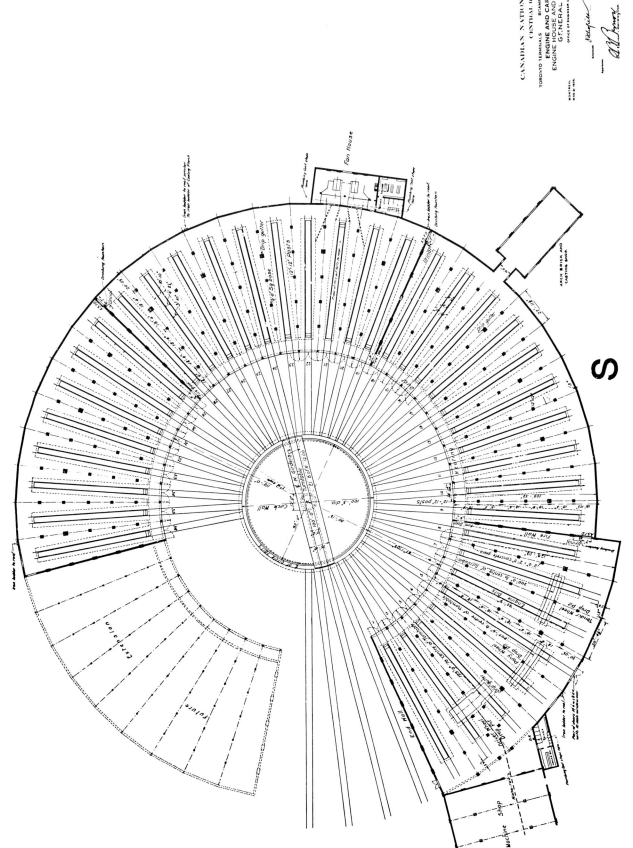

CANADIAN NATIONAL RAILWAYS
CENTRAL REGION
TORONTO TERMINALS   BRAMPTON SUB DIV   MILE 0.8
ENGINE AND CAR FACILITIES
ENGINE HOUSE AND MACHINE SHOP ETC.
GENERAL PLAN.

OFFICE OF ENGINEER OF STANDARDS

MONTREAL
MAY 1930.

Fan House

Arch Brick and Casting Shop

S

Extension

Future

Machine Shop

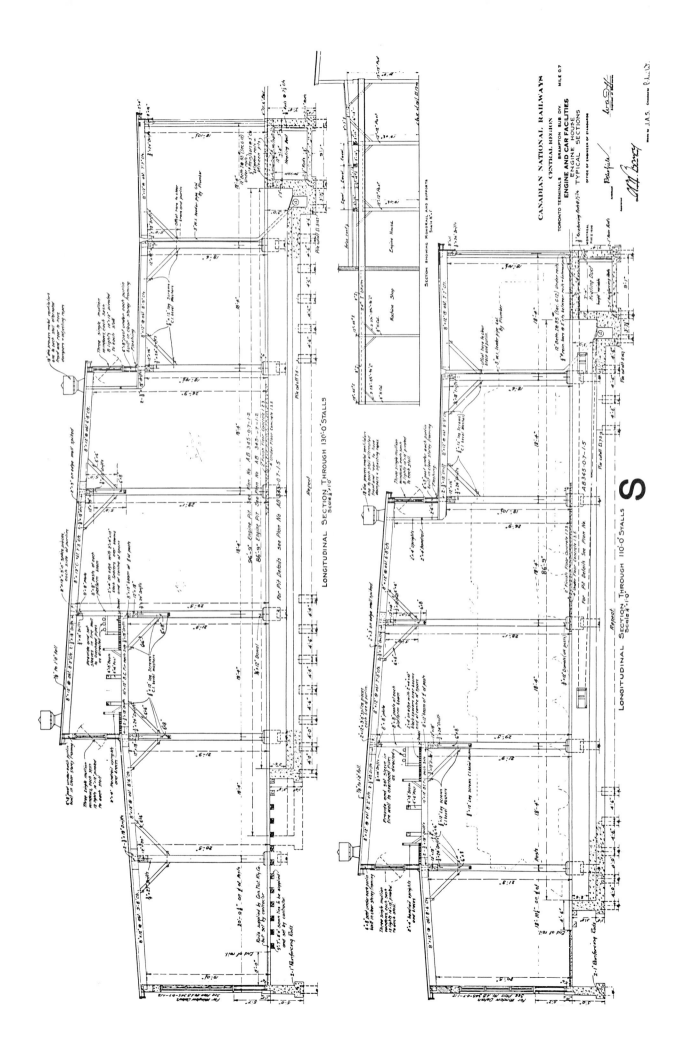

A panoramic view looking west of the Spadina bridge spanning the yards. In the foreground we see the roofs of the water tower and the ash pit house. Beyond the bridge is the coal and sanding plant with the Bathurst Street bridge and Consumer's Gas Company tanks in the distant background.

Looking east toward the Union Station and train sheds, we see the John Street signal station building standing alone beside the main track with the 1,750 foot CNR freight building behind. The roof of the locomotive house is seen in the foreground, right-hand corner. Following the skyline, left to right, is the Toronto City Hall, Bank of Commerce, and Royal York Hotel.

31

VIEW FROM THE ROYAL YORK

This photograph was taken on April 5, 1934, from the Royal York Hotel, looking west along Front Street. Included in the view is the CNR express building in the left foreground, the freight shed on the south side of Front Street which extended 1,750 feet between Simcoe Street and Pell Street, and the CNR (formerly GTR) freight sheds and property on the north side (centre left and right respectively). The sheds on the north side stood on the former site of the Ontario Parliament buildings. The southern sheds were destroyed by a spectacular fire after this photograph was taken.

THE TRIUMPH
❀ OF THE ❀
ROYAL SCOT

The Royal Scot train of the London Midland and Scottish Railway toured the Dominion of Canada and the United States of America from May 1st to November 11th, 1933, covering under her own steam 11,194 miles over railroads of the North American Continent.

During this tour the train was exhibited at 80 cities and towns and was inspected by 3,021,601 people, of whom 2,074,348 passed through the train during its five-months stay at "A Century of Progress" Exposition, Chicago, U.S.A.

Above: The title page of the official Royal Scot North American Tour booklet, handed out by the Publicity Department of the London Midland and Scottish Railway.

Harry Watson's interest in railways in general compelled him to visit and photograph the famous Royal Scot during its visit to the C.N.E. grounds at Toronto on May 3, 1933.

HARRY AND THE GANG

Left to right: Bobby Taylor, Wilf Welsh, and Harry Watson in front of CN 7501.

Left to right: Harry Watson, Jack Patterson, Bill Harvey (a great guy for tricks), Wilf Welsh and Bobby Taylor.

THE 1937 FIRE CREW

The fire fighting equipment at Spadina was a two-wheel hose rig, which carried about 150 feet of hose. The crew consisted of a nozzle man, a hydrant man, and various men who pulled the rig and made the joints or couplings at the necessary places. Practices were carried out on Front Street at Spadina, almost opposite the old British Welcome League building on the northwest corner.

During fire drill competitions, a time limit was set and the crew which went through the drill in the shortest period of time won the championship. The fire hydrant at that time was located 80 feet west of Spadina and was wide open, enabling the crew to run there, run water through the hoses and hang them up to dry.

Procedures were the same as those of a regular fire department. The competition was stiff and to only be runner-up would be a big disappointment after going through strenuous practices once a week during the summer months. The championship team won a one-year life insurance policy worth $1,000, which they were not overly anxious to see collected.

1937 Fire Crew—Spadina shops
Left to right: Jack Flaherty, Alex Reid, Louie Samarco, Eddie Sanderson, Joe Murray, Davey Curran, Jock Conlon.

Not Ashamed of the Gospel of Christ

The Railway Christian Movement

BROADCASTER

The Best of News while it is News.

FOR RAILROAD AND TRANSPORTATION MEN

Number 30　　　　TORONTO, JANUARY 1935　　　　50c a year by post. One cent through agents.

*Everybody busy—W. McIntosh, H. Watson, D. Curran, P. Cooke, G. House and
T. Falconer at work on one of the big locomotives at Toronto.*

The Railway Christian Movement was founded by William Fuller in the Depression years.
Its missionaries spoke to many railway workers across Canada and were well received.
Approximately once a month at the Spadina shops, about three missionaries would set up a
portable organ, have a hymn sing and talk with the men during lunch time.

The beautiful contralto voice of Madame Lillian Jones was enhanced by the excellent
acoustics of the roundhouse, and her performances are remembered with pleasure by many who
heard her.

THE GIANTS OF THEIR DAY

It was a great year in 1924 for the Canadian National Railways, as it took delivery of what were then the five largest locomotives in the British Empire. Including tender, locomotives 4100-4104 weighed 327 tons apiece, and were used in the Toronto area for heavy, slow speed transfer duties. The first use of Vanderbilt tenders by the CNR was on these locomotives, known as Santa Fe types.

The 4100 as she stood on display when first delivered to the Spadina yards in 1924. Nearly a ton of coal was required to line her huge firebox to a level of three or four inches. The 4100, since renumbered 4190, is now on display at the Canadian Railway Museum in Delson, Quebec.

Sante Fe type 4024 is the lead locomotive in a doubleheader pulling freight in the Toronto area. Gatehouses were a familiar sight at crossings for many years. The 4024 was built in August, 1920 and retired in March, 1955.

Sister locomotive 4035, also a Santa Fe type, but of a slightly smaller sub-class than the 4100's, is seen assisting diesel 8524 with a freight on the main line. She was built in October, 1920 and retired in July, 1957.

The 4103 as she appeared on the turntable at Spadina. Visible in the background are the tops of the Bank of Commerce, the Royal York Hotel, and the two chimneys on the City of Toronto Waterworks.

CNR 9000

The Canadian National Railway's 9000 was the first two unit passenger diesel in the world when Harry Watson photographed it in 1929. Here we see the 9000 at Spadina, with the Steele Briggs Seed building in the background.

Left to right: Duke Jones, Jock (Scotty) Williams and Harry Watson stand in front of the 9000, with three unidentified crew members in the cab above. Jock Williams was an expert on the diesel and travelled with the 9000 throughout Canada.

Harry Watson was one of the few men chosen to work on this historic locomotive. This photograph was taken through the rear of the 9000, and shows the lubricating fuel pump system, with Harry resting his arm on the auxilliary operating automatic rod.

WATER TOWER

The steel water tank at Spadina had a capacity of 150,000 gallons, and in 1927, water was pumped up to it from two city mains. Electrically driven pumps did the job and were located in the CNR pump house on the shore of Toronto Bay, just a short distance to the south.

THE DAY THE WATER TOWER CAME TUMBLING DOWN

The legend of Northern 6218, which now sits majestically in Fort Erie, Ontario, tells of when it was chosen to perform the horrendous task of pulling down the long-standing water tower in the mid-1950's.

It took only a few tugs from this giant of raw steam power, and the tower came tumbling down. What followed was a fearsome spectacle, for flames unexpectedly jumped out of the capping hole. A resultant fire continued for some time and all those present were amazed to watch the flaming water. When the flames died down, the faithful old tower was given a decent burial on site, as a tribute to its years of faithful service.

The Poage Automatic Standpipe (10'' type) is in full operation here, with a little overflow on 6234's 11,600 gallon tender. Three standpipes served six locomotive tracks at Spadina.

In the background of this and many other photographs appears the Loretto Abbey. The Abbey was located on Wellington Place, which is west of Spadina Avenue and one block north of Front Street. The Sisters of the Institute of the Blessed Virgin Mary purchased the property and commenced building a few months before Confederation. It was sold to the Jesuit Fathers in 1931, and although the Toronto Telegram bought the property in 1959, the Jesuit Fathers remained in the building until 1961. The Globe and Mail newspaper building and parking lot now stand on the site.

The close proximity of the Abbey to the Spadina shops enabled many railroaders, who so desired, to worship in the chapel after their shift.

Diesels 4472 and 8133 stand by while steam engines 5302 and 6028 pull up to the water tower. The 6028 was one of the locomotives used for the Royal Visit to Eastern Canada in 1939.

COALING AND SANDING PLANT

This structure, built in 1927, is a reinforced concrete coal and sand plant with six 100 ton circular bins. It supplied coal to locomotives on four tracks.

There are ninety steps to the top of the elevated bins, where an endless chain of 134 buckets kept six bins filled with coal from the railway's 57 ton coal cars.

Each locomotive needed eight to fourteen tons of coal, and there were about 100 locomotives serviced every day. When an engine pulled up to a bin, the chute was opened and the coal poured into the tender. Steering the coal into the allotted space was a tough, dirty job.

Locomotive sand was supplied from the areas between the circular bins and was transmitted by compressed air, which came from the concrete sand drying and storage house adjacent to the coaling plant. Tons of sand were used every day, more so when frost and snow covered the rails.

The winter months were the toughest for the men as hopper cars full of coal often came in frozen solid in below freezing termperatures.

Chute attendant George Snead improvised with specially designed (Spadina Special) heaters which he placed under the cars to melt the frozen coal in order to remove it. When the coal finally did get into the 100 ton bins, it would freeze again. Again improvising, a high pressure steam hose was used and by raising the chute door a few inches, George would shoot the steam into the coal block. It was then necessary to wait for a call from another attendant, who would be on top of the bin waiting patiently for the steam to reach the top. It was only then that they knew that the coal had thawed. This slow, time-consuming job tested the men's patience whenever it happened.

The coal chutes had to be operated during all types of weather. It was one of the toughest, dirtiest and most dangerous jobs to steer 14 to 18 tons of coal into approximately 100 tenders a day. Usually by the end of their shift, the men would be as black as the coal they were working with.

*   *   *   *   *

Early one bright morning, as one of the 5700 Hudson locomotives scheduled to go to Montreal was backing out from under the coal chute, the rope broke, the door stuck open, and 100 tons of coal buried the tender and locomotive. George Snead and the others just stood there, and with astonishment watched the locomotive being transformed into a black sculpture. When the last piece dropped, Sid Dadsworth came along with his crane and with the help of many manual shovelers, picked up the coal and transferred it into a hopper car.

Although this was not an everyday occurrence, it did happen occasionally to one or another of the many coal chutes in railroading. By the way, the locomotive didn't make it to Montreal that day!

*   *   *   *   *

Workmen's Compensation was not a fact of life during the Depression years, and decisions often involved an element of danger for the men of Spadina. On one such occasion, Herb Gough was called to the coal chute to make a repair which turned into a hair-raising experience to say the least.

A collapsed conveyor system had halted the transfer of coal to the engines and resulted in a pile of coal and coal dust at the bottom of the stairway. A new system would have to be built and in attempting to quickly clear the area of the wrecked system, Herb decided to cut it up with an acetylene torch. He soon found that powdered coal is extremely volatile, for on lighting the torch, there was a huge WHOMP! and the door exploded back. Fortunately for Herb and his helper, they were not blown into "Kingdom Come" and escaped with only minor burns across their eyebrows, face and a portion of their hair.

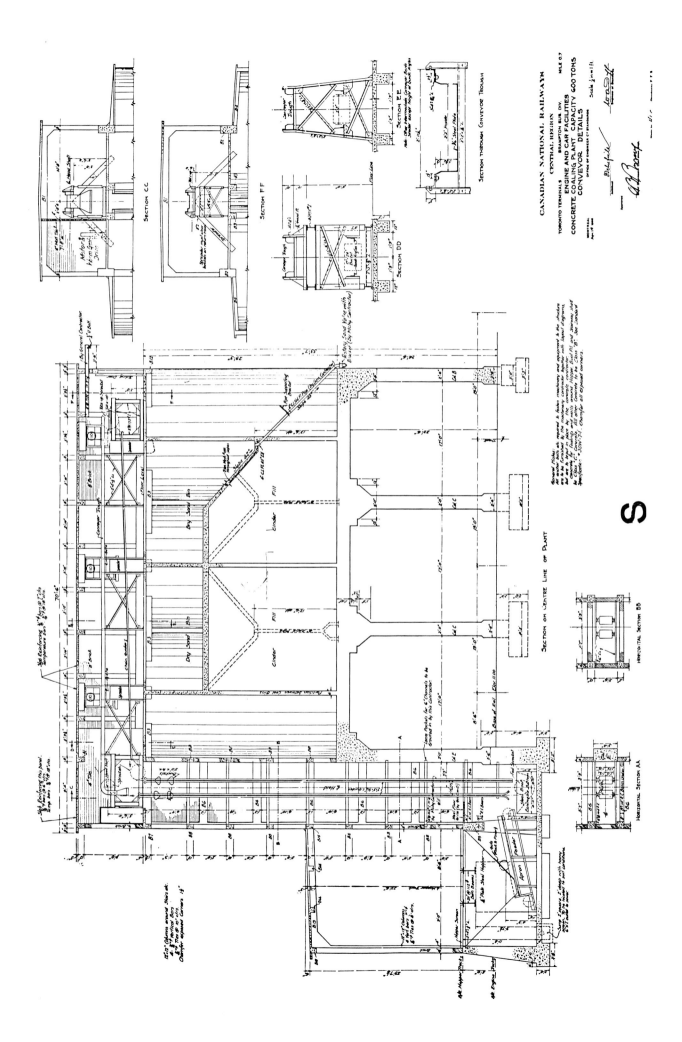

CANADIAN NATIONAL RAILWAYS
CENTRAL REGION

TORONTO TERMINALS   BRAMPTON SUB. DIV.   MILE 0.7
ENGINE AND CAR FACILITIES
CONCRETE COALING PLANT CAPACITY 600 TONS
CONVEYOR DETAILS

OFFICE OF ENGINEER OF STANDARDS

MONTREAL

Scale ½in=1ft.

SECTION CC

SECTION FF

SECTION EE

SECTION DD

SECTION THROUGH CONVEYOR TROUGH

SECTION ON CENTRE LINE OF PLANT

HORIZONTAL SECTION BB

HORIZONTAL SECTION AA

George Snead, long-time chute attendant, is in the cab of 4101 as it waits for a fill under the coaling plant.

Sid Dadsworth, crane operator, stokes up on the right while 8359 at the centre chute is being filled with coal.

6240's tender is being loaded with coal, with George Snead pulling the cord. The barrels on the platform were for safety; if the chain broke, the round weights and chains would fall into the barrel, not on someone's head!

The 5701 eases away after a fill-up at the coaling and sanding plant.

THE CINDER HANDLING PLANT

The cinder handling plant was of special design and only the second of its type to be built in Canada. The first was at the Neebing Terminal near Fort William in 1923.

The pit, continuous across five tracks, was built of concrete. There were cast iron hoppers under each track, under the openings of which a cast iron link conveyor operated, moving in a north and south direction. This carried the cinders up an incline through the ash pit house on the north side of the tracks, and emptied them into a cinder car at the north side of the house. The conveyor was driven electrically, and water was piped into the ash pit to cool the ashes.

Looking down at the ash pits and Pacific 5566 from Spadina bridge.

View from Spadina bridge, with the cinder pit area in the foreground. The buildings on the right are the stores and machine shop.

A view from Spadina bridge with 8216 and 5062 going out, while 5701 is heading in to the turntable and roundhouse.

A view from Spadina bridge with the Maple Leaf Mills elevators in the background. To the right of the photograph is the ash pit house, with its covered conveyor belt depositing cinders into the hopper cars.

EIGHT WHEELED SWITCHERS

In the winter of 1946, the CNR rented six locomotives from the Buffalo Creek Railroad to fill an ever growing need for extra motive power in the Central Region. Although not in the habit of purchasing second hand locomotives, they decided to purchase them outright in July, 1947 and assigned them to their Grand Trunk Western subsidiary. They never ran on the Grand Trunk Western rails, and while retaining the Buffalo Creek numbers at first, the CNR gradually overhauled and renumbered the locomotives.

8421 is shown in the wheel shop yard, Spadina. Built in 1923 for the Buffalo Creek Railroad as #27, and overhauled at CN Stratford shops in July, 1948, 8421 was retired in March, 1960.

The end of the line for 8418! Diesel 4510 is waiting in the background to take over. The 8418 was built in 1916 as Buffalo Creek Railroad 23, overhauled at CN Stratford shops in February, 1948, and retired in June, 1958.

CONSOLIDATIONS

The 2531, formerly Grand Trunk 667, is surrounded by memories of the past in this pre-1927 view. The old wooden water tower is barely visible behind a cloud of steam at the upper left, while the roof of the old long shop rises just beyond the tender of Grand Trunk 1279 at the upper right.

The 2631, formerly Grand Trunk Railway 635, lines up with 8448 in front of the new roundhouse. The 2631 was new in 1908 and retired in February, 1960.

A MOGUL VISITS SPADINA

"X" marks the spot! The coupler on Mogul 83 needs replacing! Number 83, formerly Grand Trunk Railway 1003 and CN 905, was built in 1910 and retired in January, 1959.

Mogul 83 is seen here coupled to work train 50484. That's Loretto Abbey in the background again.

PACIFICS AT SPADINA

Harry Watson at the controls of Pacific 5292.

Here the 5594 leaves the train shed of the old Union Station. The engine, built in 1911, was formerly Grand Trunk 221 and was retired in February, 1960.

Pacific 5031, built in 1912, was formerly Grand Trunk 101 and retired in March 1960. The original Loretto Abbey is again seen to the right in the background.

5296 stands over the ash pits with the ash pit house to the left. She was built in July, 1920 and retired in September, 1961.

The 5267 faces a standpipe with the water tank behind. Formerly 495 of the Canadian Government Railways, this engine was built in 1912 and retired in March, 1960.

Grand Trunk 5582 is seen here during a visit to Spadina. She was retired in November, 1955.

Mikado 3249, formerly Canadian Government Railways 2849, challenges another locomotive face to face at Spadina. This gladiator retired in December, 1958.

Mikado 3419, formerly Grand Trunk Railway 514, is seen with a caboose in the Toronto area. The locomotive was built in 1913 and retired in November, 1957.

MIKADOS

The 5700 gets a steam wash. Her driving wheels are 80''. Retired, November, 1961.

Hudson 5702, shown here on the turntable at Spadina. She was retired to the Canadian Railway Historical Association Museum at Delson, Quebec in September, 1960.

Hudson 5701 as she pulls away from the Spadina turntable in May, 1936. Retired, March 1960.

Hudson 5701 pulls away from the coaling plant. Note the addition of wind deflectors (Elephant Ears) on the sides.

It's a smoke break for Harry!
Left to right: Jack Flaherty, Harry Watson, Don Willis, and Pete Ferguson with the 5701.

Nineteen railroaders pose on the 5704, complete with smoke deflector, as she stands on the Spadina turntable shortly after delivery from the Montreal Locomotive Works in 1930. She was retired in 1961.

The 5703, with an experimental smoke deflector, is shown here with the Spadina water tower in the background. She was retired in June, 1961 and was renumbered 5700 for display at the National Museum of Science and Technology, Ottawa, Ontario.

MOUNTAINS

The old coal chute provides a backdrop to this view of the 6033, which places the photograph in the pre-1927 era. The engine was built in 1924 and retired in 1961.

Three buddies pose in the cab of 6033, on which they have just completed work. Harry Watson looks through the window, while Davey Curran stands over Charlie Pile.

The 6023 is being positioned on the turntable by the operator, seen in the hut on the left. This engine was built in July 1924 and retired in March 1959.

Mountains 6033 and 6031 nose out of the open doors of the roundhouse. This picture was taken in April, 1956.

ROUNDHOUSE DOORS

A new design of door with structural steel frame is seen here. The outside members are small four inch I beams with welded joints. This four inch thickness provides an opportunity for double sheathing and air space, and is sufficiently stiff to resist warping. It is much lighter than many other steel doors which were designed in the past. Hinges with adjustable pins have been provided which assures proper swinging.
Canadian Railway and Marine World, *November 1928.*

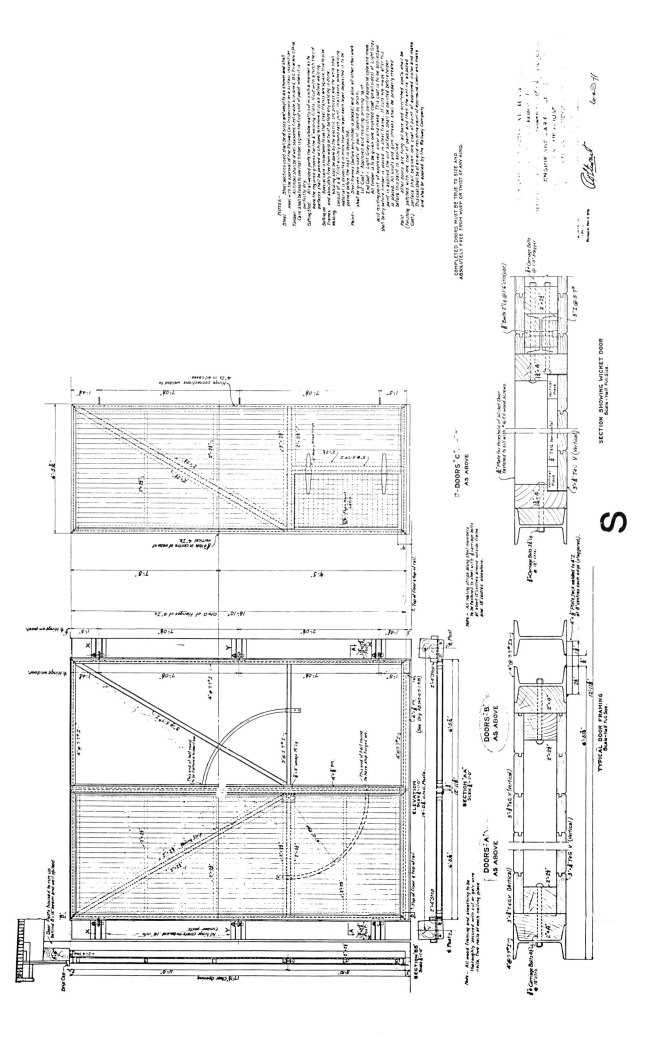

COMPLETED DOORS MUST BE TRUE TO SIZE AND
ABSOLUTELY FREE FROM WARP OR TWIST OF ANY KIND.

SECTION SHOWING WICKET DOOR
Scale - Half Full Size.

TYPICAL DOOR FRAMING
Scale-Half Full Size.

S

STREAMLINED NORTHERNS

The Canadian National Railways took delivery of five U-4-a 4-8-4's in June and July of 1936. These streamlined locomotives were researched by the Canada National Research Council in 1931, to resolve the problems of smoke flow and wind resistance.

Built for speed with 77'' drivers, the 6400's served the Montreal-Toronto-Sarnia Corridor and were very colourful with their green running boards, cab and tender. The smokebox front and running gear were black, while the boiler jacket and casings were of planished steel.

Retired in 1960, only the 6400 remains preserved, at the National Museum of Science and Technology in Ottawa.

Here we have the Canadian National's elite locomotives 6400, 6402 and 6401. Of the four gentlemen standing in front, Alex Reid on the right is the only one who could be identified.

The 6400 meeting her public in Toronto at the foot of Simcoe Street in June, 1936.

The 6401 is coming east into Danforth Station (Toronto) under the Main Street bridge. In the background, centre right, a locomotive being watered from a standpipe is in view.

A profile shot of the 6401 shows the yard engine 8341 in the background.

ROYAL LOCOMOTIVE FOR THE ROYAL TRAIN

A complete overhaul of the 6400 was ordered in preparation for its appointment to pull the Royal Train, during part of the King George VI and Queen Elizabeth Royal Tour in May and June of 1939.

Bill (Buck) Harvey and Bobby Taylor were chosen to head up the team to do the job, and work commenced in March, 1939. By the time the job was completed, two months of constant work by these two men and many others had passed, and everything in the engine had been examined from stem to gudgeon. In fact the whole engine was taken completely apart and put back together again. Rods were stripped off, valves and pistons taken out, rings examined, and everything that there was to look at was carefully checked by these men of the Spadina shops.

The 6401 preceded the Royal Train on the route and pulled a big diesel electric generating car which provided power for the Royal Train when it stopped on a siding out of town. Behind the generating car were the sleeping and dining cars, which were provided for the press and officials covering the tour.

The 6400, built in June 1936, is shown as she has her picture taken in the Spadina roundhouse on a time exposure of 10 seconds. The Royal Coat of Arms, mounted under the headlight of the Royal locomotive, comprised approximately 25 pounds of solid brass. The 6400 was retired to the National Museum of Science and Technology in Ottawa, Ontario, in June, 1967.

MAJESTY IN WAITING

Here are the Royal machinists who travelled from the Spadina shops to London, Ontario, on the Royal Train. They are Bill (Buck) Harvey, machinist, left, and Bobby Taylor, machinist's helper. In 1984, Bobby Taylor still has the overalls he wore, neatly pressed, in a dresser drawer.

6400 in full view on the turntable at Spadina shops.

"Attention Please!—All eyes towards the camera." The men of the roundhouse stand smartly for inspection with the Royal locomotive. Left to right: Rosie Ferry, Bill McIntosh, Cliff McBride, Jack Flaherty, Ralph Robbins, Davey Curran, Alex Reid, Bob Bowman.

The Royal Crest spruces up the tender of 6400. The engineer and fireman wait while a machinist makes a last minute inspection on May 26, 1939.

The crowds wave goodbye as the Royal Train pulls away from Toronto on its way to London, Ontario.

"A Job Well Done." Royal locomotive 6400 sits in profile on the turntable at the Spadina shops after pulling the Royal Train.

The 6401, pilot locomotive for the Royal Train, is getting the finishing touches.

NORTHERNS

Northern 6121 is shown as she is being positioned on the turntable at the Spadina shops. Oldtimers remember an unfortunate accident that involved the turntable at Spadina. It seems that the turntable was lined for the wrong lead track and a locomotive was run headlong into the tiny control hut. Since the hut had only one door, the operator was unable to escape. An emergency door was added shortly thereafter.

Northern 6156 is seen here pulling into Danforth Station, Toronto, from the east. Her next stop will be Union Station. The 6156 was built in May, 1929 and retired in October, 1961.

The 6201 is travelling east and entering Danforth Station, Toronto, under the Main Street bridge. The 6201 was built in June, 1942 and retired in March, 1960.

"Hurry up, we're all steamed up and ready to go!" Harry Watson looks out of the cab of 6220, heading to go under the Spadina bridge. The 6220 was built in September, 1942 and retired in July, 1961.

The 6237 pulls her train of coaches along the main line. She was built in August, 1943 and retired in February, 1960.

The 6245 enters Danforth Station, Toronto, travelling west. This locomotive was built in September, 1943 and retired in September, 1961.

Harry Watson takes it easy in the cab of Northern 6246, while his co-worker completes the final touches. Seen here with the coal plant in the background, 6246 was built in September, 1943 and retired in September, 1961.

The 6300 poses for her portrait in the Spadina yards.

WOMEN AT SPADINA

Railroading was traditionally considered a men's world, but during World War II, approximately 25,000 CNR employees left the company to serve in the Armed Forces. To replace some of those who worked at the Spadina yards, women were hired to work on the engines for the first time, primarily serving as wipers and oilers. Here we see just a few of these wartime employees, as they gathered around a couple of spotless Northerns that had just been given their considerable attention.

BULLET-NOSED BETTYS

Twenty new semi-streamlined Mountain type locomotives were delivered to the CNR in 1944. Nicknamed "Bullet-Nosed Bettys", number 6060-6079 were easily distinguished by their flanged stacks, conical noses, pilot-mounted aftercooler housing and running board skirts. They were clean of line and easy to maintain.

The 6071 and 6076 pose for a formal portrait beside Spadina's water tower.

The 6060 can now be seen at a railway museum near Edmonton, Alberta. Here she poses at Spadina when new in 1944.

The 'powers that be' inspect the new 6060.
Left to right: Len Gallaway, locomotive foreman, Spadina shops; J.W. Bailey, superintendent, motive power; W. Sealy, general superintendent, motive power; J.F. Pringle, Vice-president; R.C. Johnston, general superintendent. The photograph was taken in 1944.

"A Living Locomotive." The entire Spadina shop day shift is assembled on the 6060 during a campaign promoting War Savings Certificates. According to an article in Keeping Track, January/February 1981, CN employees became known as the largest purchasers of Victory Bonds and War Savings Certificates of any industry in Canada.

Here we have "Bullet-Nosed Betty" 6064 with her engineer and fireman on the through tracks at Union Station. The tracks are 1,500 feet long and are covered by the low style, two track span train shed. The 6064 was new in October 1944 and retired in March, 1960.

Checking the size of the main crank pin is generally the machinist's job. A new floating bushing will be made up from a four-way casting. This day the size was taken in style, by Foreman Bob Withrow.

The 6063 hauls her passenger train coming east, after passing under the Bathurst Street bridge. Next to the bridge in the background is a Consumer's Gas tank. The 6063 was built in October, 1944 and retired in December, 1961.

The 6066 is heading a doubleheader with Hudson 5701 west of Spadina bridge. She was new in November, 1944 and retired in June, 1962.

Mountain 6077 is easing away from the coaling plant, while Pacific 5281 looks on.

A FUTURE AUTHOR VISITS HIS DAD AT WORK

On one of their many visits to the roundhouse during the summer holidays, teenagers Ron Watson and friend Fred Quance visit Ron's Dad and the 6071.

STRIKES—THE MEN

"We don't want to die with our pie in the sky." The picketers proclaim the AFL's answer to management's claims of excessive demands. Here posing in front of the entrance to the CN property at the southeast end of the Spadina bridge, are left to right: Art Parson, George Alexander, Bill (fast Mac) McIntosh, (seated) Herbie Gough (leader of the pickets for the day), Jimmy Perry, George Gilles, unidentified, Charles Polito, Charlie Pile, Reg Pricely, Gord McNulty, Percy — —. The building in the background of this 1950s photograph is the telegraph stores building.

Strikers proclaim their demands in front of the commissary building.

STRIKES—THE ENGINES

All was strangely quiet in the Spadina yards as the strikers paced back and forth carrying their placards. Their ears perked up as they heard the impossible; a locomotive in motion, a violation of the strike! They couldn't believe it, but sure enough the clatter and track-rubbing squeal, familiar to the workers in the yards on other days, got louder and louder. They looked around in confusion. Management investigated the source, but found nothing.

Later, a supervisor admitted that he had played a recording of a working engine over the public address system. It proved that the CNR had very good loudspeakers, but the practical joke enjoyed by so many was not thought to be funny at all by others.

A view from the Spadina bridge, looking southeast toward the roundhouse, as life stops in the yards during a strike. In the right foreground is a good view of a hopper stopped under the ash pit house, where it received a load of cinders.

BACK TO SCHOOL

Conversion from steam to diesel was a massive project, not only for the railway company but for the individual railroader who had to be retrained, and who must have said many times, "Let's just keep the steam."

Seated in a passenger car which has been converted to a classroom are, left to right: Ray Price, Sid Sterling, unidentified, Leo Daignault, Stan Goddard Jr., Dean Gibson and Harry Watson. Standing—Harold Atherson, instructor.

"Now that we're graduates from Diesel school, Harry, let's convert this diesel to steam." Harry Watson, left; Fred Burrn, right.

DIESELS INVADE THE YARD

Spanking new General Motors passenger diesel 6537 is seen here with the Spadina bridge in the background. It won't be needing the services of the coaling plant on the left.

This view, taken from the Spadina bridge in November, 1958, is looking over the cinder plant toward the turntable. Diesel engines are beginning to make inroads on the Spadina scene.

The 9098, a General Motors A unit, is seen here surrounded by steam locomotives.

The 6501 is lined up beside a rival at Spadina.

Hidden under the coaling plant, steam locomotive 7520 is kicking up smoke, perhaps in protest that the diesel in the foreground is taking over some of her duties.

Oop's! Steam yard locomotive 8448 is outnumbered by a line-up of diesels.

Harry Watson shaking hands with Jack (Windy) Phillimore beside General Motors passenger diesel 6533, one of the new fleet purchased in 1958.

Stall 33 frames the back of General Motors road switcher 1722, while the sun catches 6504 as it rests in stall 32. This picture was taken in May, 1956.

A workman is busy breaking up the turntable wall with a pneumatic drill. A few stalls remain in service.

Temporary scaffolding has been erected to simplify the breaking up of the turntable wall.

TURNTABLE REPAIRS

Summertime at the roundhouse meant another little job to do. Periodically, the rails leading from the stalls to the turntable would expand, catching the turntable and preventing its free turning. Alex Ferguson or one of the other men would take a cutting torch and cut an inch or two off, to even it up. Two or three weeks later, the same thing would happen and another inch would be cut off. The extra length was due to heat expansion.

Major turntable repairs were undertaken on numerous occasions, and disrupted the processing of the locomotives. Plans were formulated for ongoing maintenance of the engines, which would therefore have to be completed in the outdoors. Somehow, Harry Watson's station usually managed to be located under the Spadina bridge. If it was raining, hot or windy, Harry would be protected from the elements.

Pacific 5578 looks on as the turntable repair work continues. The section of the roundhouse seen here includes stalls 1 to 8 (right to left), with a firewall just visible between stalls 8 and 9. Each stall is 130 feet deep.

Taken from the roof of the roundhouse in November, 1958, this photograph looks west toward the Spadina bridge. The water tower and 120 foot flood light tower take centre stage as new track is laid on the turntable deck.

A very busy day in the Spadina yards! The water tower dominates this scene taken from the Spadina bridge and looking east. The stores building is shown in the right foreground.

Whenever the turntable broke down or was being repaired, one of the cinder pits became a temporary shop pit. Ready to get to work are, left to right, back row: Joe Ledeman, Fred Booker, Jack Flaherty, (Mickey) Grunick. Front row: unidentified, Al Murray, Jack Fairney.

"Smile, we're getting paid for this!" Part of the roundhouse crew poses for a picture, in front of their temporary quarters during turntable repair. Left to right: Tommy Lewis, Len Samis, Bill Bassest, unidentified. Kneeling: Sammy Palmer, unidentified, Bill Hillman, Harry Watson, unidentified, Elwood Robinson, George Johnston.

Working in the outdoors while the turntable was being repaired, Mikado 3272 and Mountain 6069 on the left, face Hudson 5700 and a tender on the right. Note the small crane with rubber tires, used for transporting heavy parts and machinery.

Eddie Sanderson with one of the small shop cranes at Spadina.

Ted Doran, one of the "chief lubricating engineers, 1st class," is seen operating the grease gun. A supply of grease sticks is available at hand on the trolley to the left-front. When this job was completed, the locomotive was ready for its run.

The roof of the machine shop provides the site from which this 1958 photograph was shot, which looks northwest. Steam and diesel wait side by side in the yards for the turntable to be repaired.

The view facing northeast from the roof of the machine shop, takes in the Bank of Commerce building and the Royal York Hotel in the background, while steam and diesel sit side by side in the foreground.

TURNTABLE MISHAPS—STEAM

Early one morning, 6230 made a fast exit from the roundhouse, and Harry Watson was on hand to record the scene. This U-class 4-8-4 was built in January, 1943 and retired in April, 1960. Her tender held 11,600 gallons of water and 18 tons of coal, when it was on the level.

TURNTABLE MISHAPS—DIESEL

"What do we do now?" Switcher 7990 presents a problem as it sinks into the turntable pit. From the photo collection of Harry Watson, but one of the very few in this book not taken by Harry himself. Credit Jerry Diachun for this sequel to Harry's previous steam turntable mishap views.

PATCH THIS UP?

This photograph of a Mikado type locomotive was taken in July, 1955 and no one knows for sure whether she was repaired or sent to the scrapper's torch.

SHE WAS STILL BRAND NEW

Six men view 9005 and a B unit which were caught coming and going. The passenger car shop is in the background.

CNR MUSEUM TRAIN—1953 TO 1957

Although actually hauled by Mogul 674, the Canadian National Railways' Museum Train featured two veteran locomotives. The 247, built in 1894 for the Grand Trunk Railway, was one of the few saddle-tank engines to run on Canadian lines. Number 40 was an American type 4-4-0, built in 1872 at the Portland Works.

These photographs were taken during the train's visit to Toronto in the mid-1950's. Some of the Museum Train's exhibits and equipment now rest on display at the National Museum of Science and Technology in Ottawa, Ontario.

ROUNDHOUSE FIRE

Early one morning in the 1960's, a major fire broke out at the Spadina roundhouse. All the diesels were removed by the quick-thinking railwaymen, before they sustained any major damage. Here we see the aftermath, with some of the Toronto firemen making sure that the fire is completely extinguished.

THE GRAVEYARD

Northern 6215 in her heyday, full of life and ready for another trip on the rails. She was built in August, 1942.

The 6215 is seen during the winter of 1960, showing her age and covered with a mantle of snow. She was officially retired in June, 1961. Note the 120 foot light standard superimposed on the 160 foot radial brick chimney of the roundhouse.

Obviously an emotional scene for Harry Watson to photograph, Northern 6174 sits among other idle locomotives on a siding. She was built in April, 1940, and retired in November, 1961.

Mountain 6021 was new in June, 1924, retired in November, 1959, and awaits her fate in February, 1960.

A view of the old steam locomotives at Spadina, waiting to be sent to the big roundhouse in the sky. Their modern diesel successors are probably gloating, and can be seen on the move in the background.

REPRIEVE FOR 6213

Northern 6213 was sent to the scrap line, at Bathurst Street in Toronto, in the spring of 1960. She languished there for months, ready to be sent to the scrapper's torch at the Reclamation Yards in London, when Bobby Taylor received a phone call from the boss. The order was to return the old girl to the shops, because, "She is going to the Exhibition grounds."

On retrieving the old engine, they found that many of her parts had disappeared during her stay in the scrap line. Those who worked on her had to borrow from other engines to make up the loss. When the work was finally completed in July, 1961, she was pushed up to the Canadian National Exhibition grounds, where she remains on proud display to this day.

Northern 6213 poses for a final portrait in the Spadina yards.

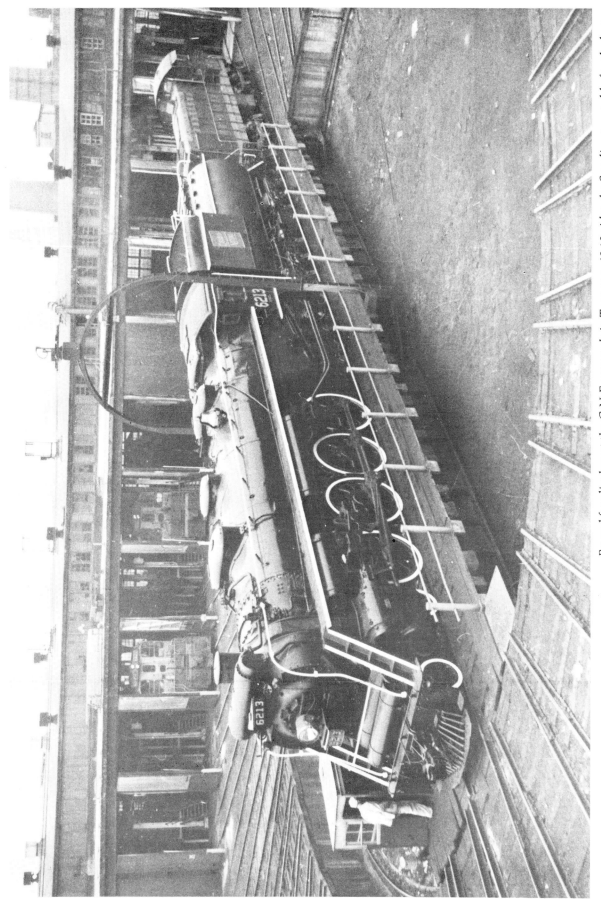

Bound for display at the C.N.E. grounds in Toronto, 6213 rides the Spadina turntable for the last time. Engineer Jim Marley and fireman Roger Gellel felt sad, as they "pushed another piece of railway history" away from the shops that she knew so well.

FROM SCRAP TO MASTERPIECE

Ten Wheeler 1325 was built in 1910 by the Montreal Locomotive Works for the Canadian Northern Railway. She was authorized for renumbering to 1533, in 1956. United Scale Models Inc., and the New Hope and Ivyland Railway in Pennsylvania, U.S.A., purchased her on December 1, 1962 and took delivery after considerable refurbishing was completed by the Spadina shop crew.

Beginning the process. The grime of idleness on Ten Wheeler 1533 is being cleaned away by a steam wash, as diesel 3102 regards the scene.

1533 on the turntable, about to enter the roundhouse for her overhaul.

Harry Watson in the pit, giving a preliminary inspection to the 1533.

A masterpiece completed, ready for shipment to her new home.

THE FAMOUS 6167

Northern 6167 was built in March 1940. After the end of regular steam service, she was retained by Canadian National Railways as an excursion engine from July, 1960 until September, 1964, at which time she was formally retired to permanent display near the station at Guelph, Ontario.

Her years at the head of railfan excursion specials made 6167 one of the most photographed locomotives on the CNR. Her longevity was made possible due to the efforts and knowledge of oldtimers like Harry Watson and his co-workers at Spadina.

Northern 6167 sits alongside Ten Wheeler 1533 inside the Spadina roundhouse.

The 6167 eases out of the roundhouse with Bobby Taylor posed between two unidentified helpers. Joe Boyle stands below them on the pilot steps.

Northern 6167 waits for the final checkup before leaving on a steam excursion, while a few railfans give her the once-over. The Royal York Hotel is visible in the centre background.

A WORTHY REPLACEMENT

Northern 6218 was chosen to replace 6167 as the CNR's steam excursion engine. Here we see Harry Watson in her smokebox, getting ready to pull leaking boiler tubes. Leaks in the units under test were identified by the boiler foreman, and their numbers can be seen chalked on the running board steps to Harry's right.

Fresh from her overhaul, Northern 6218 stretches her legs in the Spadina yards. Her number plate has yet to be installed. Now retired, she is on permanent display at Fort Erie, Ontario.

The first fan trip runs of 6218 were doubleheaded, in the company of retiring 6167, on September 26 and 27, 1964. These trips ran respectively from Toronto to Scotia return, and Toronto to Paris return.

MEN HAVE LAST TRIPS TOO

Traditionally, the last run of a railway engineer is recognized by installing a large sign or banner on his locomotive. Here we see engineer Sam Cherry in the cab of Northern 6141, after 45 years of service.

Sam Cherry came to Canada from Scotland as a young boy, and worked on the CNR out of Belleville, Ontario, until the mid-1950's. He was remembered by the machinists at Spadina as having the most beautiful (and readable) handwriting on his locomotive reports.

THE MEN OF SPADINA

Left to right (standing) Harry Watson, Davey Curran and (sitting) Jack Conlon, Sid Robinson proudly display their 25 year certificates from the International Association of Machinists.

Good food, good drinks, and a good union meeting! Left to right: George Armstrong, Alex Harris, Al White, Joe Albert, Harry Moon, Fred Johnston, George Bunny (far right). It was a good party, that's why we could only identify a few.

A strictly business Union meeting. Seated at the tables flanking chairman Fred Johnston are Gord Stewart and Dave Dalziel on the left, with George Johnston on the right.

Wash-up! Only Herman (Mucker) McGregor would take time to look at the camera.

Harry Watson, with longtime co-worker Alex Ferguson on his right, posing on the 3121.

Testing the oil and water from the diesel locomotives was done in this room. Shown here are left to right: Harry McRae, Joe Leedham and Mike Breen.

"The last few minutes of the working day are the longest." Here the men wait for the time clock to jump.

Just imagine punching this clock for forty years or more! Left to right: Alex Procenko, Ian Orr (summer student, son of Hugh Orr), Sid Powell, Art Parsons, Alex Ferguson, George Johnston.

Spadina "Board Room Meeting", to discuss the paperwork policies! Left to right: Tommy Andrews, Morrison McCullough, Harry Grunnell, Leith Tilson, Len Buckley, John Scott, Unidentified.

Foreman Bill Carnagie, machinists Morris McCullaugh and Harry Gummel, worked on the steam generating units which heated all diesel passenger trains. The board behind them was used for checking off each unit as it was inspected on arrival. If defects were found, Bill may have had to assign extra men to do the job.

HARRY WATSON AT THE CONTROLS

"If you can fix them, you can drive them!"

CALLING IT A DAY

July 21st., 1966.

Mr. Chairman and Fellow Workers,

I thank you very much for your kind complements on behalf of the Company and the Union.

I don't wish to take up much of your time, so that you can get back to your work in order to keep the wheels rolling. The company needs the money and so do we.

During my 43 years of service at Spadina, conditions have not been of the best. Wages were not always the best. Lay-offs were drastic from time to time, including ten per cent cuts in pay cheques. I'm pleased to notice in the past few years, wages and conditions have improved and so has the business between Unions and Managements. On this matter, there is a lot of work to be done in the future owing to automation. In this, I wish you both much success.

As for myself, I have enjoyed my work in spite of sometimes unpleasant conditions. The bigger the job, on steam locomotive or diesel, the better I liked it. I always found it interesting, also the fellows I have worked with. It's sometimes said - "A man happy in his work is a happy man anywhere." My time has come. I have to leave you on account of my age. I would have liked to have carried on. I feel fine, but I, like others at my age have to go by the Company and Union rules. Here's my parting wish to the Company and all the members of it's staff, particularily you all at Spadina Round House I know so well - Better and safer conditions and prosperity during your service with the C.N.R.

Yours very truly,

N. Watson

The 8514 forms a backdrop for a farewell handshake between Harry Watson and Phil Embury, Foreman. In Phil's speech at the retirement day lunchroom ceremonies, he said "Happy retirement, Harry. All the best to Spadina Shops' only resident photographer."

Canadian National Railways

Room 1450,
20 York Street,
Toronto 1, Ontario.
18 July, 1966.

Mr. H. Watson,
153 Parkmount Rd.,
Toronto 6, Ont.

Dear Mr. Watson:

It has come to my attention that after being in Company service since 26 April, 1923, you will be retiring on 31 August, 1966.

May I take this opportunity to extend to you my sincere wishes for a long and happy retirement. The Railway is most appreciative of your many years of loyal service. The change to a life of leisure will no doubt allow you to develop your hobby of photography and the other interests you have enjoyed over the years.

Once again best wishes for health and happiness in your retirement.

Sincerely,

Manager.

Harry Watson, setting the valves on an MS10 diesel yard unit.

Harry Watson is seen here standing beside an MLW diesel engine.

Well, that's it! The end of the line! Harry Watson posing with 6761 on his last day.

Harry Watson checks good old steam locomotive 6218 for the last time on July 21, 1966.

A production co-ordinator was responsible for material for the incoming and outgoing locomotives. He had to forecast the regulatory inspections for the coming month. Tommy Haddon was seen in one of Harry Watson's earliest photographs in 1923, as he posed with the Bull Gang. He later became foreman, then production co-ordinator, and it is in this capacity that he bids farewell to Harry.

THE DAY THE ROUNDHOUSE DOORS CLOSE

It is recognized that the railway lands on Toronto's waterfront are an important part of Toronto's heritage. The changes in the area since the first settlers established themselves on Toronto Bay is dramatic. The coming of the railway to Toronto had caused its citizens to turn their backs on the waterfront as the dirt and grime of the steam era succeeded in disfiguring its natural charm. What became evident to the author as he spoke with the men who worked at the Spadina yards during the steam era was that these men, who made the railway their career, were unique in their contribution to a way of life in the midst, and in spite of, the degradation of the area. The excitement of the railways was theirs, for it was they who ultimately made it happen. Without their expertise and know-how, the great iron horses could not run, and this fact was reflected in each personality.

The time is past, and the landscape is fast changing again, but it is hoped that as Toronto's railway lands disappear from the waterfront, that precious moment in time when men worked together in a common cause, will be remembered as a valuable part of Toronto's heritage.

The line up! A variety of tender rear-ends on display in their stalls at the Spadina roundhouse.

The 6262 enters Danforth Station, Toronto, travelling west. Built in February, 1944, 6262 was retired in February, 1960.

ACKNOWLEDGEMENTS

I would like to thank my mother, Mrs. Beatrice Watson, for her support, encouragement and for the valuable background information that only the wife of a railroader can give; my son Chris, who sorted hundreds of negatives; and my wife Verna, not only for her patience and encouragement, but also for editing and typing the manuscript.

Although the men of the Spadina shops held a variety of positions, management and workers shared a common goal. They were, in the best sense of the word, a fraternity, exclusive in its dedication to maintaining the locomotives in their care to the best of their various abilities. The incredible memory of the men I interviewed was invaluable, be it in putting a name to a face sixty years later, or describing a long forgotten story. In fact many of the stories told, while providing insight and entertainment, could not be included in the book. They were the mysteries, and mysteries they must remain.

Following is a list of those who contributed information and stories:

	Service	Date Retired
Herbie Gough	50 years, 5 months	October, 1968
W.R. (Ross) Chalmers	49 years, 3 months	February, 1975
George Snead	47 years, 11 months	August, 1968
Bobby Taylor	45 years	— —, 1964
Sid Cope	44 years, 6 months	June, 1968
Phil Embury	43 years	June, 1984
Bill Bayliss	42 years	June, 1983
Bill Carnegie	40 years	April, 1976
Alex Ferguson	40 years	June, 1968
Leith Tilson	39 years	April, 1983
George Armstrong	38 years	April 1976
Roger Gellel	37 years	Still working hard
Total	516 years, 1 month	

Additional information and data came from Mrs. Frances Rowan (wife of the late Bill Rowan), Hugh Orr, Ralph Hay, and Dave Dalziel.

Thanks to Miss Esther Fuller, daughter of the founder of *Christian Transportation Incorporated*, formerly *The Christian Broadcaster*, and to John Pringle and John Clark for information about the publication and its involvement with the men at the Spadina yards.

I wish to thank the Canadian National Railways for the excellent co-operation afforded me in all the departments I visited and especially the following people:

J. Norman Lowe, Historical Research Officer, Montreal;

Clifford Dunn and Ken Billings in the Toronto engineering office;

M.E. Mathews, Public Affairs, Toronto.

To the City of Toronto, a sincere thank you for their enthusiasm and co-operation, in particular; Mayor Arthur C. Eggleton's office, Mr. David Goyette; Archives, Victor Russell, Karen Teeple, Elizabeth Cuthbertson; Urban Design Group, Ken Greenberg, David Dennis.

Also thanks to:

> The Canadian Railway Museum, Delson Quebec;
> The Archives of Ontario;
> The Public Archives, Canada;
> Metropolitan Toronto Library, Baldwin Room (Canadian History), Business Department;
> Scarborough Public Libraries, Agincourt Branch;
> North York Public Libraries, Fairview Area Branch;
> Peter Mykusz, Photographer, Scarborough;
> Brian Ashton, for valuable sources;
> Ken Richards, for his references of diesel locomotives;
> Jack Long for map reproduction;
> Alan Robinson for his encouragement and support.

I would like to thank Ralph Beaumont and The Boston Mills Press for seeing a potential book in hundreds of photographs, and for helping to make what was to me a major undertaking, a pleasurable experience.

Brand new Northern 6261 is idling with Spadina bridge in the backgound.

BIBLIOGRAPHY

Andreae, Christopher
Railway Heritage Study in Toronto
London, Ontario, Historica Research Limited, 1983

Artibise, Alan F. J. and Stelter, Gilbert A.
The Canadian City
Toronto, MacMillan of Canada, 1979

Clegg, Anthony and Corley, Ray
Canadian National Steam Power
Don Mills, Railfare Enterprises Limited, 1969

Cooper, Charles
Narrow Gauge For Us
Erin, Ontario, The Boston Mills Press, 1982

Dorin, Patrick C.
Grand Trunk Western Railway
Seattle, Washington, Superior Publishing Co., 1977

Goad, Charles
Insurance Plan of the City of Toronto
City of Toronto Archives

Legget, Robert F.
Railways of Canada
Vancouver, Douglas & McIntyre, 1973

Martyn, Lucy Booth,
Aristocratic Toronto
Toronto, Gage Publishing, 1980

Metropolitan Toronto Library Board (Reference Library)
Canadian Railway & Marine World
1906 through 1936

Stevens, G.R.
Canadian National Railways – Vol. I
Toronto, Clarke Irwin, 1960

A rare photo is this view of CNR electric storage battery car 15801, a forerunner of today's Dayliners, seen here with a snowplow attached on its visit to Toronto.

Spadina bridge and the water tower form a backdrop to 4101, 5701 and 7150.

Harry Watson at the controls of a diesel.

CANADIAN · NATIONAL · RAILWAYS
CENTRAL REGION
TORONTO TERMINALS   BRAMPTON   SUB. DIV.   MILE 0.7
ENGINE · AND · CAR · FACILITIES
JULY   1926

S

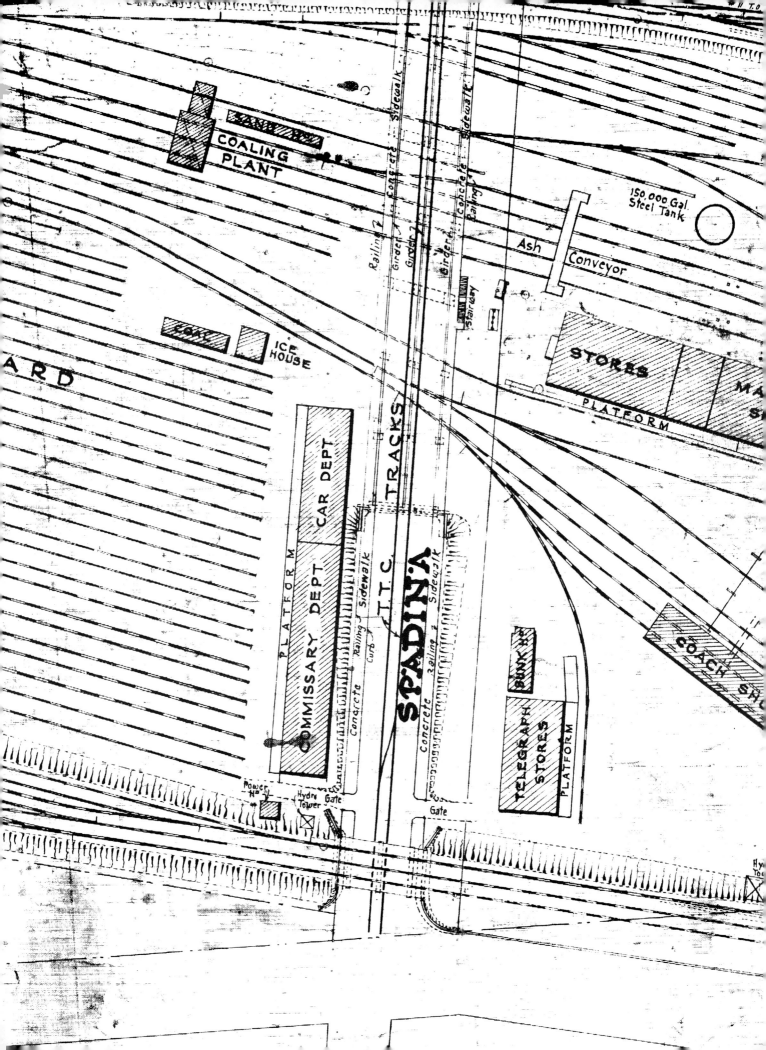

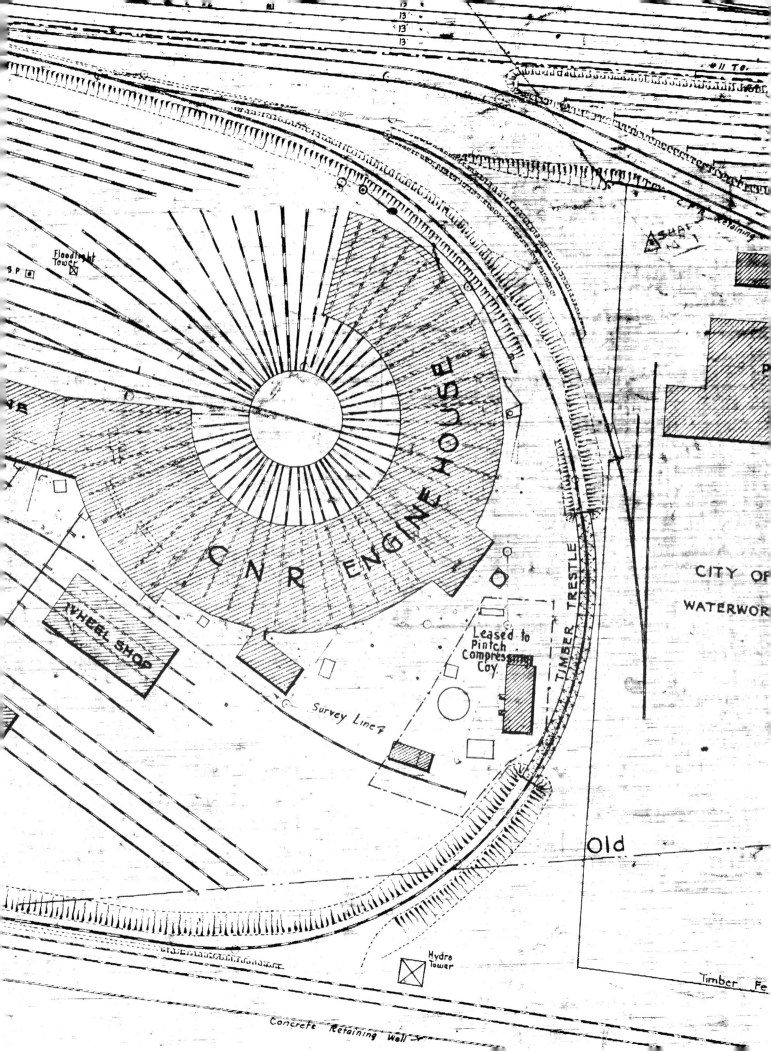

CNR ENGINE HOUSE

WHEEL SHOP

Floodlight Tower

S.P.

Survey Line

Leased to Pintch Compressing Coy

TIMBER TRESTLE

CITY OF
WATERWOR

Old

Hydro Tower

Concrete Retaining Wall

Timber Fe

13
13
13
13

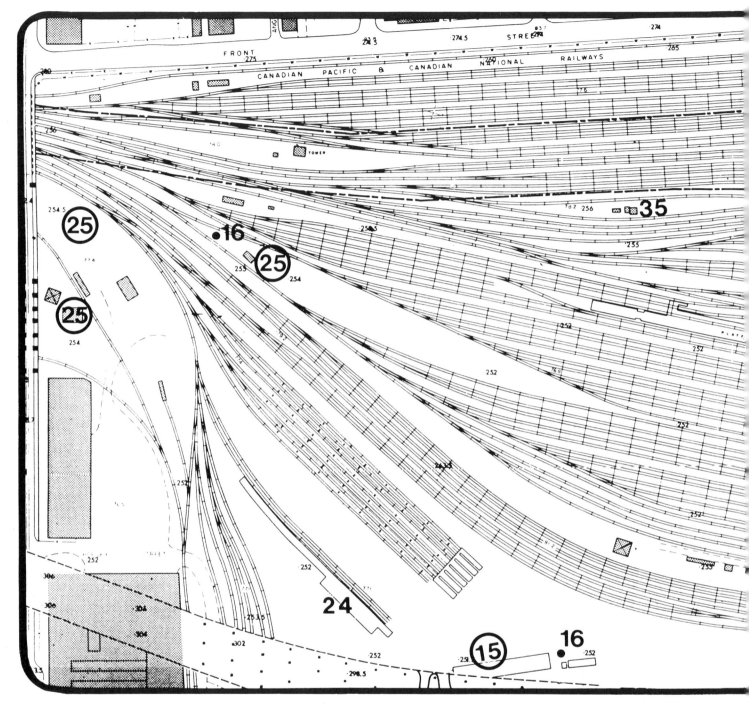

○ **FEATURE REMOVED**

CANADIAN NATIONAL RAILWAYS
— SPADINA YARD —

1. coaling & sand plant
2. cinder handling plant
3. standpipe
4. water tank
5. turntable
6. locomotive house
7. machine shop
8. stores building
9. wheel shop
10. passenger car shop
11. Bunk houses
12. Passenger Car Yard

13. Commissary
14. Window Repair
15. Freight Car repair
16. Yard Lighting
17. Heating Supply (not mapped)
18. Through Freight Track
19. Run Around Track
20. Fuel oil tank (not mapped)
21. Substation building
22. Ice House
23. Garage
24. Storage & Mill building